LOOK & FIND OUT

Ocean Animals

by Alice B. McGinty

Scholastic Inc.

How do animals live in the Ocean?

Cold and pressure

Deep water

Can be very dark

Dolphin

Mammals need air to live. Mammals that live in the ocean must get oxygen from the air.

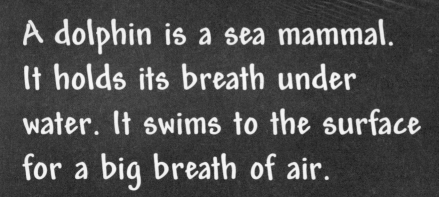

A dolphin is a sea mammal. It holds its breath under water. It swims to the surface for a big breath of air.

Manta ray

The manta ray has fins like big wings. The manta ray flaps its fins up and down to move through the ocean.

The manta ray can turn somersaults. It can even leap out of the water!

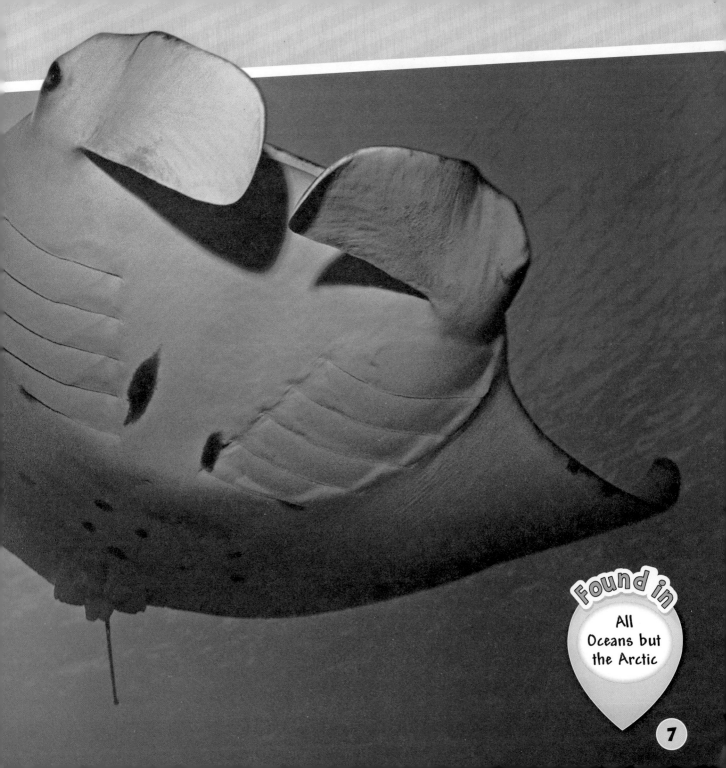

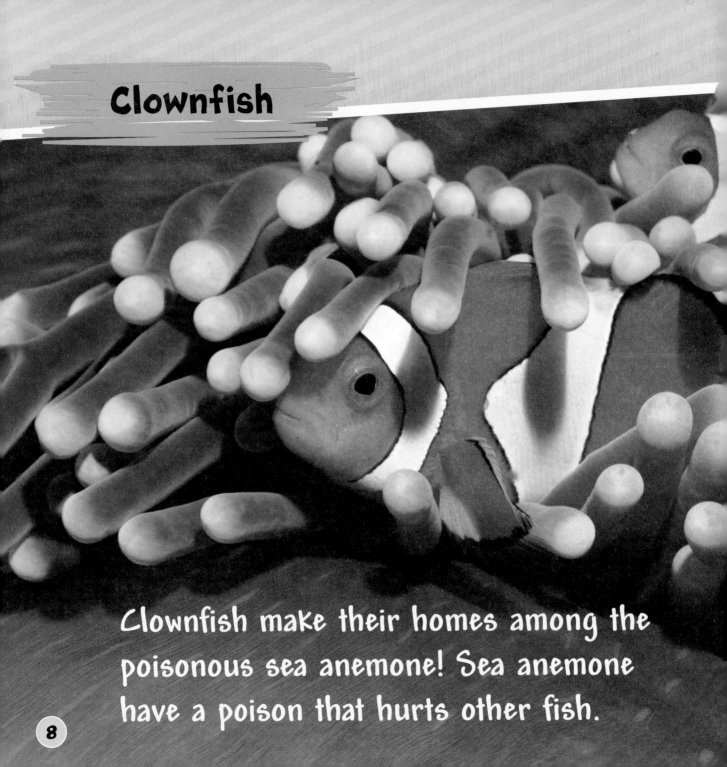

Clownfish

Clownfish make their homes among the poisonous sea anemone! Sea anemone have a poison that hurts other fish.

A special coating on the clownfish protects it from the poison. Since other fish stay away, the clownfish is safe in its home!

Found in
Indian and Pacific Oceans

Anglerfish

The anglerfish lives in the deep ocean. It is very dark in these deep waters.

This anglerfish has a built-in flashlight on its head! Other fish swim over to see the light. Then the anglerfish eats them!

Gray whale

Ocean animals have many ways to find food. This gray whale opens its mouth. Water rushes in. A screen in the whale's mouth filters tiny sea plants and animals from the water.

The food stays in the whale.
The water goes back into the ocean.

Lionfish

Ocean animals must protect themselves from predators that want to eat them.

The lionfish stays safe in three ways. It blends into its surroundings. If a predator comes near, the lionfish spreads its fins to scare it. If the predator comes closer, the lionfish stabs it with poisonous spines. Ouch!

Find Out More

A dolphin breathes from a blowhole on its head. It keeps the blowhole shut underwater. When it reaches the surface, it exhales to clear water near the hole.

The manta ray has big lobes on both sides of its wide mouth. It points the lobes forward while swimming. When it feeds, the lobes direct water into its mouth.

The clownfish forms a protective layer on its body after the poisonous anemone stings it. In an aquarium with no anemone, the protective layer disappears after a while.

Glowing bacteria live at the end of the anglerfish's "pole." The fish and bacteria help each other: The bacteria get a place to live; the fish gets light to catch food.

The screen, or baleen, that many whales use to filter creatures in the water is made from the same substance as hair.

A lionfish spreads its fins wide to show its red and white stripes. The stripes can confuse predators and make the lionfish look larger.